For Love's Sake

Nikki Delgado

BookLeaf Publishing

India | USA | UK

Presentation by *BookLeaf Publishing*

Web: www.bookleafpub.com

E-mail: info@bookleafpub.com

ISBN: 9789357446549

First edition 2022

DEDICATION

To my parents Maria and Ronald, if not for your boundless love and support, I wouldn't be who I am today, the writer I am today. To Jayden, Loya, and Santiago for the friendship and happiness you've gifted me. To my dog Sugar, your adorable presence is always healing; I look forward to many more years of your tail wagging and whining. Thank you all, and I love you all dearly.

ACKNOWLEDGEMENT

Thank you to the BookLeaf Publishing team for this fantastic opportunity, along with the patience and support they've given me during the book-making journey.

PREFACE

A walking tragedy,
A one-woman dance party,
A 19-year-old not ready for reality,
But she can't shut up about love.

To Our Tomorrow

Hi.

The greeting we exchange means a tomorrow,
And hopefully a forever,
For your presence means destiny
And my words, I believe, will echo for an
eternity.

I look forward to our now, our future, and
everything in between,
If you'll have me, of course

Memories of Gold

The smell of car exhaust and coffee was always accompanied by
The sounds of laughter too loud and secrets too toxic.
But It was all so right.
It was all golden…
Somehow.

As the screeches of metal chairs
Fused with the echoes of Eagle Rock's afternoon streets
I would then sit down and take a sip of my mocha frappuccino,
Thinking to myself,
"Please, let us stay this way."
Because it all felt too precious.
It felt too good to be true.
Yet they're still here, all of them.
Or rather, we're still here, all of us.
Through the teenage angst (that refuses to leave)
And the pain you'd only expect to see in some raunchy and cliche 6 seasoned drama,

We've gone through things both stupid and
outrageous.
Teenagers shouldn't actually live through those
romanticized struggles.
But that made us realize we didn't need much
more than what we already had.
Ambition,
Determination,
Laughter,
And Us.

After some time,
The smell of car exhaust and coffee was
accompanied by
The sounds of laughter too-loud,
Memories both toxic and sweet,
The shared anxiety of a future uncertain, but
hearts connected as one.

We were golden,

We're still golden,

We'll always be golden.

You've Got Me Enchanted

Laughter heals the soul
You prove it to me when I'm with you
With every pitch change, a blossom blooms
The melody of your voice
Lulls the sun
Rouses the moon.
Laughter heals, but yours...

Yours is magical.

More than Sunshine

I can see the grimace you make
Each time you slap that same ol' facade of
Sweet summertime and saccharine acts of
self-sacrifice.
So,
I know you don't understand when I say
You're more than sunshine.
Although the sun could never hope to compete
with your true smile,
You are you.
The you that cries in silence,
The you that screams in isolation
You, who has long forgotten what it means to be
vulnerable
Without the fear of being judged or ridiculed.

You're more than sunshine,
You are you,
And I'm here for you, too

Lovely, As Always

Boundless, you're as lovely as you deserved to
be loved.
You're making me a certified romantic since
There will never be enough poetry,
That can help me articulate what you deserve to
hear
That can capture the universe you show me
And I know my incompetence handicaps my
endless love,
But that will never inhibit my attempts to
express these affections to you.

A Wish, A Cry, A Prayer

Too often do the shooting stars I see only come
in showers.
And I can only watch on as I become drenched
underneath
Sorrowful starlight;
Wishing for twinkling rain to never fall again,
If it came from your miserable night sky

Tonight Under Moonlight

May the moon be my witness
With the stars by my side
We only have this moment
Our love
Found in the night

Daybreak Brings Heartache

As the sun rises once more
With the stars long gone
Time ticks once again
Our love
Lost to daylight

You've Gone To Galaxies

You've must've been embraced by the stars
Because never before have I seen
Your smile so shimmering
Your eyes, so iridescent
Your soul so filled with wonder
Your heart so at ease
You're so lovely...

And the distance between us has never been
greater.

While I've remained here on earth,
You've traveled across planets,
Nebulas,
Galaxies,
And tonight, as I look to the sky,
I know our time together has come to an end.
But I still see a time that glitters
Just like you, now.

The Journey Has Just Begun

My biggest adventure was becoming yours
With my treasure being you
But this surely isn't the end of our journey
No, this is merely the start.
We have the rest of our lives together, after all.

I can't promise rainbows and sunshine 24/7
But I can promise you a partner in crime.
Through thick and thin,
Dragon slaying or fairy catching,
A ride or die,
All the cliches you can think of and more.
I'll go through it all with joy, as long as you're by
my side.

What new treasure will this grand adventure
bring? We'll find out soon enough...

So,
Are you ready?

Flower Language;
For You

Tilted to the left, trembling with anxiousness, is
my outstretched hand.
(Red columbine)
This hand holds all my unspoken thoughts,
(Motherwort and pansy)
And as I pass them to you,
I ask that you refrain from plucking petals or
even pressing your lips to a flower,
(Escholzia)
and to please consider each dear thought of mine
carefully.
(Wild daisy)

With this confession of love,
(Moss rosebud)
I'm asking you to dance with me.
(Viscaria oculata)
To fly with me.
(Venus' car)
I'll offer my all,
(Shepard's purse)
If it means that you'd think of me.

(White clover)
If I were to say that the color of my life was you,
(Coral honeysuckle)
Would you be mine?
(Four leaved clover)
You see, this heartache has only one cure: to be
by your side.
(Swallow-wort)

You have me trapped, I'm you're captive.
(Peach Blossom)
If the only way to achieve freedom
(Water willow)
Is to declare war against you,
(Wild tansy)
Then I dare you to love me.
(Tiger lily)

I'm determined to win
(Purple columbine)
And have you return my love to me.
(Jonquil)

Irreplaceable

You don't remind of home,
For you are my home.

We won't grow old together,
You make me young.

I never believed in soulmates,
Until I met you.

And as long as we live under the same sky
We'll never be apart.

I'll always find you
So please, wait for me.

For the Marvel That Is You

As effortless as a waterfall
With the same amount of force too,
Fingertips that bleed magical melodies
A voice honey-soaked and aging like fine wine,
A mind as playful as your laughter is contagious
And eyes that clearly showcase your
unbreakable will
How lucky I am to have been able to meet you.

Loving You/Me

For all the praises, affections, and compliments
That I can screech with my whole chest and bust
a lung,
For the swelling in my heart and flames that lick
my soul sparked by indignation
For everyone else except for myself,
Not gonna lie... That's pretty wack.

From the pressure of societal beauty standards,
internalized misogyny, cultural gender roles, all
topped with imposter syndrome,
It's amazing to think about how much love I
have for anyone,
Considering the walking tragedy that I am.

It's a process, really, to accept what your loved
ones see in you.
And sometimes...

Sometimes I can see it too.

It's hard to recognize the awesomeness of
yourself.
To realize all the work you've done to make it
this far.

To notice that you're alive, experiencing love,
sadness, happiness, anger, everything under the
sun and beyond.
To see that you too, are every bit as magical as
the world around you because
You
You are a part of this world.
You are a being made up of stars,
With a bleeding heart, curious soul, open mind
This is your story
And It's all so beautiful, so raw,
It's you.

You deserve to be screeched about,
To be sang praises to and be cared for.
I/you should love yourself/myself as much as
I/you love you/me.
It's truly wack otherwise.
Seriously.

Smile

Take a lesson from Nat King Cole because
sometimes
You gotta smile for yourself, even if you're this
close to snapping.

You gotta hug yourself,
Pat yourself on the back,
Treat yourself to that kid's happy meal you've
been craving lately,
Or treat yourself to the latest episode of your
most recent obsession,
Maybe get that thing you saw on Amazon last
time you were browsing.
Get some dopamine for yourself when no one
else will.

When the universe seems to be having a field
day with you,
Smile.
As ridiculous as it sounds, as difficult as it may
be,
The sun will always shine.
You'll still be here, and,
In the end, you'll figure everything out.
You always do.

You've done your best, you'll continue to do so,
and I couldn't be more proud.

Extinguished

No amount of care could bring back the star fire
that fueled her lips.
It made her voice pour out like the falling
feathers of a phoenix,
Majestic,
Bright,
Searing.
Now, in a world without a sun,
All that's left are the dying embers of a soul
extinguished.

Burn

I wish I could tattoo my name on your tongue
So you could never forget the taste of what you
lost.
But you don't deserve to be graced with my
name,
Much less any part of me.
Instead, I hope you've been burned with the taste
Of a fire so angry, so alive
You regret ever having taken a bite.

1:38 AM - Call Me a Wizard

I'm no genius.
I'm no wizard of words,
Mage of the pages,
Einstein of the book spines;
I ain't got no cultural, historical, cool & funky
hits,
The revolution has yet to start up here (in my
mind),
But I AM me, and I write for the sake of writing.

My writing can be clean-cut fresh, accompanied
by a voice like thunder,
Complimentary to the power I speak.
In here, I have the chance to be the winds of
change,
To be a hero and fly,
See worlds unknown or become a god in my
own right,
I could craft my own scriptures and enforce my
own commandments.

The neglected emotions and unnecessary
complexities of everyday life unravel Becoming
the embodiment of chaos but it allows me to
write.
I'm no genius, but my love? It's genuine.
My writing?
It's me.

Four-Legged Miracles

Fuzzy and furry four-legged best friends,
Irreplaceable and oh so sweet,
Where would families be without you?
I couldn't fathom a life without seeing
Your tail-wagging, butt-dragging,
tongue-hanging, sweet and friendly self.
I'm sure plenty others agree, that you and your
kind are too precious.
We really aren't worthy of your unconditional
love,
But we'll be sure to do the same for you.
Our cute babies, our little menaces, our
four-legged miracles.

Tenfold

Calloused hands and wrinkled brows
Accompanied by smile lines,
Awe-inspiring, all of it.
Proof of a life hard-lived and enduring,
Yet, people as fascinating as you,
Chose to love me.
Since, giving birth is not what makes parents,
parents.
It's the true love they hold for their children.
And as a result, all I've ever received has been
Warmth, comfort, support; a home.
I'm spoiled because of it, I know.
But one day, aside from all the love I have for
you both, now,
I plan on giving it back tenfold, not as a thank
you, for although I am grateful,
You deserve it.
You deserve even better, so I will be too.
I just have to get this "adulting" thing down first.
But look forward to it.

To Our Forever

Like the ocean, I wave
With the sun, I shine
Carried by the wind,
Hi.

Our time together may be ending here,
But we still have these words, forever.

So as the tide recedes, so do I
With the moon, it's time
Taken by the wind,
Goodbye.